MUSINGS AND MEMORIES

A Collection of Poems by

Sue Hollings

A.H. STOCKWELL
PUBLISHERS SINCE 1898

Published in 2024 by
Sue Hollings
in association with
Arthur H. Stockwell
West Wing Studios
Unit 166, The Mall
Luton, Bedfordshire
ahstockwell.co.uk

To all my friends and family, with love

Contents

Musings and Memories

To My Girl Far Away

(1974)

How can a man who loves you so much
live for so long without feeling your touch?
It isn't easy, I can tell you that now.
But to the voice of experience I'll willingly bow.

Experience says: apart is the test,
to see if it's you who she loves the best.
I don't doubt experience because it is wise,
but what I would give to gaze into your eyes.

I know it's not long 'til we meet again,
so I will be patient, and wait until when
I can hold you so close in my arms, so strong and tight;
and I won't leave again, either to work or to fight.

Us

(1974)

Each time I look at a certain star,
I think how lucky we both are;
to have each other to love and hold,
and say "I love you" a thousand fold.

For my part, our love is such bliss;
I live from touch to touch and kiss to kiss.
We have something that's deep and strong;
it's something concrete, a real tight bond.

I think it's possible for you and I
to be just like that star in the sky.
That star will never lose its shine,
and like you, love, it will glow for all time.

Who's Kidding Who?

(1991)

As I climb the stairs to go to bed
I shake my poor befuddled head;
my teeth in a glass, wig on a stand,
corset released... oh ain't that grand!

Elastic stockings, veins encased,
gratified to be released.
Wrinkles, dimples, ample flab;
don't pinch an inch, just grab a slab.

I'm no page three girl, as you can see;
just a homely lady of forty-three—
age that is, not children born!
It's bad enough with the bits that are worn.

My shoulders are droopy, my bottom has sagged;
I'd fail an MOT with the bits that I have lagged.
My plumbing is rusty, could do with repairs.
Got it, flaunt it? I wouldn't dare!

I must be a reject from my parents' genes;
I've inherited leftovers, or so it seems.
No sylph-like curves or freckles for me... no!
Just dandruff, halitosis, spots and bo.

When I go to bed, all I have is a book,
photos and memories of how I should look.
I'm a recycled teenager preserving myself,
so I'll just carry on sitting here on the shelf.

Reflections

(2004)

Gathering dust upon the shelf
are the diaries I wrote about myself;
full of stories, out of date,
youthful adventures and their fate...

Like the time we met by the station clock,
or ran to the harbour to see the ships dock.
Our dads weren't aboard this one, they said;
the war had claimed them: *England's dead.*

Mothers with ration books, going to town
for vegetables; "Good for you, get 'em down."
Sharing the bathwater in front of the fire;
grey shabby clothes drying on lines of wire.

Having left school and looking for work,
we weren't allowed to dally and shirk.
We were the heads of the family now;
blisters on hands and a hot sweaty brow.

We managed though, through thick and thin;
tough as old boots was our leathery skin.
Sitting back in my armchair softly reposing,
feeling my eyelids gently closing.

Thoughts of all the years gone by;
another chapter in life's cloudy sky.
No more heartache, pain or sorrow,
for all the memories will be gone tomorrow.

Summer's Evening

(2004)

Looking up into a clear blue sky,
the birds are flying extremely high.
Will-o'-the-wisp floats on a gentle breeze;
harmonious sounds of the buzzing bees.

The trees provide a panoply of shade
as I sit and drink my lemonade.
The dog lies panting at my feet,
the picnic untouched - it's too hot to eat.

I close my eyes and drift away,
dreaming of paradise I'll find one day.
As dusk descends on my reverie,
I'm encompassed by an insect menagerie.

The village bells release their toll
as I make my way down from the grassy knoll.
The sky is turning iridescent shades of red;
promise of more summer days ahead.

The Parting

(2005)

She watched him go, she watched him walk,
he wouldn't even stay to talk.
The crying came, the crying went;
deceit and lies were never meant.

Just like the raindrops, her tears fell;
what would happen, who could tell?
All on her own once again,
wondering just what might have been.

Years together and months apart;
she held him - the dearest - in her heart.
It was a misunderstanding; she told him so...
but he was determined, he decided to go.

She closed the door to the midnight air,
and snuggled up in the fireside chair.
Overcome by the flames and candlelight,
she whispered to him, *"my love, goodnight."*

Bliss

(2006)

When you look back all those years ago
and see what you've achieved,
time is a great healer...
or so you would believe.

It was said on that wedding day
"For better or for worse",
so don't worry when the padlock rusts
on the chastity belt and purse.

Don't sit there counting long grey hairs
or wrinkles, rolls of fat;
just open another Sanatogen
and be happy with the fact—

—that you've the rest of your years together
for the virtues of married bliss.
So put a battery in the zimmer frame,
and a pucker in a kiss.

Polish up the wooden leg,
perm the second hand wig,
nip down to the Darby and Joan club
for some Phyllosan and a cig.

Lasting Love

(2011)

Together at last for your Autumn years;
no regrets, no time for tears.
Destiny ruled that the fates should allow
you both to share this happiness now.

Never-ending time to sit and recall
the past, the present, memories all.
Laying the foundations for the rest of time;
together, forever, in happiness sublime.

Don't let go; hold each other tight,
enveloped in a halo of contentment bright.
Set yourselves up for the winter years;
God bless, good health to you both my dears.

Like

(2019)

Like the sunshine you come and go;
like the oceans you ebb and flow;
like the moon you wax and wane;
like the dark clouds you sometimes rain.

Like the love you have given to me;
like being together forever be;
like the sweet thoughts from your heart;
like we will never be apart.

Life and Love

(2019)

I would give you the world
if I could hold it in my hand,
but that is quite impossible;
I knew you would understand.

Instead, I could give you a piece of my heart,
as I know that we will never part.
After all, a piece is better than none—
as this relationship has just begun.

So when we have been together for years and years,
all through the good times and the tears,
we'll add up the good times, take away the bad;
be there for each other and never be sad.

The Little Blade of Grass

(February 2020)

The green is looking wonderful,
the woods are running true;
the clouds are looking ominous...
can we see this match right through?
The teams are casting all their jacks,
they're rolling very fast
until one jack stops suddenly,
against a little blade of grass.

Number one says, "This looks bad;
I'll move it with my wood."
Skip says, "Then go for it—
would be clever if you could!"
Number one then sends his wood,
but the bias is all wrong;
the wood goes straight across the rink
to the ditch where it shouldn't have gone.

Number two says, "Let me try;
I'll move the little blighter."
Yet he has even less success,
his woods are even lighter.
The reluctant jack just stays there—
stubborn as an ass,
totally immovable
—by that little blade of grass.

Skip says, "Come on, sort this out;
we haven't got all day!
The rain clouds are looking darker,
there's not much time to play."
At last the match is over,
all twenty one ends are past.
We could have won this easily,
but for a little blade of grass!

Dawn

(With Keith Hollings, March 2020)

I was sat upon my bed with his grundies on my head,
trying to stop the glare of early morning sun.
I knew I'd look a plonker, I knew I'd look a twit...
but I thought I'd have a little bit of fun.

When he walked in through the door, his eyeballs hit the floor;
he didn't know whether to stand there, laugh or cry.
He sat down on the bed, took the grundies from my head
and proceeded then to slide them up his thighs.

I couldn't look away, I had to sit and stare
at the sight that befell my watery eyes:
on his bum there was a dimple, and at the side of that a pimple
that was growing to a great enormous size.

The spot was ripe for squeezing, but I had a funny feeling
that he wouldn't be very happy if I did.
I thought I'd let it grow; through his pants it wouldn't show,
and over time - through friction - it would rid.

So if the sun is in your eyes, use a curtain or a blind;
save the grundies for the purpose they were made:
for a bloke to cover his cluster, or use them as a duster
when the edges have become a little frayed.

We always have a laugh when he stays over at my gaff,
whether in bed, watching telly or playing a game.
Wouldn't life be dull, like a knotted ball of wool,
if each and everybody was the same?

The Seasons

(With Keith Hollings, June 2020)

The seasons of the year all roll into one,
and you never know if they've been or gone.
The weather maps all blend together;
it doesn't matter whatever the weather.

An Indian summer in the autumnal days
filling the air with warm sunny rays;
winter's footprint will show its face
as the cold and wet appears with grace.

After the winter we have the spring,
and up in the trees the birds will sing.
April next with its seasonal showers,
but rain is needed to water the flowers.

Not far off is the longest day,
only a few weeks after May.
Farmers in fields for the haymaking deed,
storing it up for the winter feed.

Not long now to the nights getting darker,
the autumn equinox a seasonal marker.
That year went quick... where did it go?
Soon we'll be covered in crispy white snow.

Proposal

(With Keith Hollings, June 2020)

Now we've gone an' done it,
I can't believe it's true!
We'll have to fix a time and place
for us to say "I do".

I'll make him very happy,
I'll even kiss his bum...
but I hope I don't get pregnant;
I'm too old to be a mum.

The wedding'll be in a church somewhere,
I hope it's on the level.
I cannot climb a lot of steps
even though they lead to heaven.

The reception'll be in a nursing home
just in time for tea;
they'll all be stood in a snaking queue
to empty their bags of pee.

With the stairlift overloaded
and zimmers everywhere,
we'll quietly sneak out the open door
and stroll in the cool night air.

Matron calls for bedtime
and we furtively disappear,
but they all stand by our bedroom door
to see what they can hear.

But we'll be very quiet
Not even the sound of a mouse
We daren't do it noisily
We'd waken all the house.

We'll walk out in the morning
to pick a honeymoon,
but at our combined ages
we'd better do it soon.

The Greenkeeper

(With Keith Hollings, July 2020)

The greenkeeper's job is an onerous task;
he doesn't have time in the sun to bask.
Cutting the grass, killing the weeds;
these are just two of his numerous deeds.

Feeding, re-seeding, watering well;
some might say it's a job from hell.
He tries his best but can't please all;
he gets the blame for a wayward bowl.

The committee have bought him a Tonka toy;
he pushes it round like a proud little boy.
It feeds the grass to a plush shade of green
to make it the best rink you've ever seen.

He's got all the chemicals to feed the grass well,
but he has to be careful 'cause they're toxic as hell.
He wears a Hazmat suit, all yellow and bright;
if you didn't expect it he'd give you a fright.

He clears out the ditches and the rubbish that's there,
blown in by the winds that don't really care.
It's sometimes the seeds off the trees in the spring
and sometimes a feather from a bird on the wing.

Now and again the pheasant appears,
strutting across like he has done for years.
If this green carpet is fit enough for a bird,
the green keeper has done his job to the word.

Birthday Ode

(2020)

Like a cue for a song
I'll pen you an ode;
something quite simple
so your mind won't explode.

I'll use all the little words
so they're easy to read;
nothing too difficult
so concentrate and heed.

Can you hear the postman
knocking on the door?
He has lots of cards for you
full of best wishes galore.

You are getting old and past it;
now everything is downhill.
Just enjoy this lovely day
if you've the patience and the will.

I had better get a move on;
this pen is nearly through.
All I wanted to say was
"Appy burfday to you".

Tinnitus

(January 2021)

When you're sitting in the silence of an empty room
and all you can hear is your breathing,
add onto that the tinnitus noise
and your patience will soon be leaving.

The whistles and screams that seem to appear
will override the normal sensation
of listening to ordinary everyday sounds
that fill your day with elation.

Tinnitus will blight your life,
not like a cold or a cough;
the only sure-fire cure for this
is to cut your flipping head off!

The Ferry (Room for One More)

(February 2021)

We fancied a trip to the Isle of Wight, as many people do,
so we purchased ferry tickets and we waited in the queue.
We could see that the vessel was filling to the core,
but bung-'em-on Bob shouted, "Room for one more!"

We were last on the ferry, we were right at the back
And we heard the ramp close with an audible smack.
We could feel the boat moving out into the Solent,
We were on our way, lets savour the moment.

The crossing was smooth but can sometimes be choppy;
if you get a rough trip it could spill your coffee.
But on this occasion we were there in a trice;
the surroundings, the weather and the crew were quite nice.

A few days later it was time to come back,
our goody bags laden with this and with that.
The trip coming home was as smooth as can be,
with the sun shining bright on a mirror flat sea.

We'll visit again, maybe later this year,
and sail on the ferry from Lymington Pier.
We'll queue in the line with our eyes on the door
and hope to hear Bob shout, "Room for one more!"

My Best Mate Jan

(February 2021)

She's a formidable lady is my best mate Jan,
fussing over everyone, doing what she can.
Jan has many ailments - far too many to mention;
I wish I could heal them all, put them in detention.

She can be stubborn, she can be shrewd;
don't get on the wrong side of her when she's in a foul mood.
But, on the other hand, she's there for you
if you're down in the dumps or feeling blue.

True friends are hard to find;
you know the ones I mean—
the friends that listen and don't judge
and take you under their wing.

I've known Jan, my best mate,
for quite a number of years.
We've shared the good and bad old things,
the laughter and the tears.

So when you've found you soul-mate,
look after them good and true.
If you don't, my best mate Jan
will be coming to look for you.

National Coastwatch Institution: Eyes Along the Coast

(March 2021)

It's blowing a gale outside again;
the clouds are black and grim.
Not the sort of weather
for a craft to be sailing in.

The larger craft like liners and tankers
are sheltering in the bay,
well and truly anchored;
let's hope they stay that way.

When the weather is nice and the sun is bright,
it's beautiful in the bay;
you can see for miles and miles
as the vessels go on their way.

For all the attractions of the sea,
it can be a dangerous place.
Every tide could tell a tale
of events that have taken place.

But from our lookout on dry land,
we'll watch for mishaps and failings.
And, if needed, we'll call out the lifeboat
so you can enjoy future sailings.

That's why we're here; it's what we do,
we watch out for unlucky events.
Make sure you have a phone with you;
it's only common sense.

Please be careful out on the water,
it can catch you unawares.
But someone is watching over you
to allay your fears and scares.

Is It Me?

(April 2021)

What was that you said, my dear?
I didn't hear you very well.
Please don't mumble in your beard
and you'll be as sound as a bell.

Is it you who can't speak clearly,
or has my hearing gone to pot?
Everything sounds like cotton wool,
or else I have lost the plot.

I've tried all things, like olive oil
and even the odd handstand!
But I don't feel any different;
I really don't understand.

Perhaps it is me in denial;
your speech is obviously good,
so I will just have to try harder
and listen as well as I should.

Meal-Time Adverts

(May 2021)

Have you ever wondered,
whilst sitting down to eat,
the problems of a leaky bladder?
So please use *Always Discreet*;
they have a supa-dupa lining
to collect unwanted wee.
I'm sure this info goes down well
whilst drinking a cup of tea.

And then onto the main course,
perhaps a sausage or two...
just to be shown the right way
for you to clean the loo!
The dishwasher and washing machine
don't get off scot-free,
as there are products for them to smell nicer,
all while sitting down for tea!

Advertisers pick their moments
to offer their advice,
but do they have to do it
while I'm eating chicken and rice?
How about a musical interlude?
That would be a treat;
not all these pesky cleaners and scrubs
when sitting down to eat.

Service with a Smile

(With Keith Hollings, June 2021)

We'd seen the Ford dealers here in Torbay
so we called in there the other day,
just for a look to see what's about
when (not) by surprise the salesman came out.

He walked towards us, bearing a grin,
and asked us what we were interested in.
We said, "This one please: the Ecosport."
He said, "I'll get the keys; I think I ought."

He went to the office and was back in a flash;
we could see in his eyes, he was sensing cash.
He opened the car and my partner got in;
she said, "I want it, please; to refuse would be a sin."

We went to the office to complete the deal;
It went so smoothly it didn't seem real.
Details taken, trade-in agreed;
Well done Ford for efficiency and speed.

A few days later, the car was ready;
we drove it home, nice and steady.
We put it in its parking place
and a neighbour saw it, with a smile on her face.

"Where did you get it?" My neighbour enquired,
"It makes my old car look very tired."
"We bought it at Vospers, it was done in a trice;
the salesman was Niam, he was ever so nice."

So if you are thinking of changing your car,
then call in at Vospers, it's not very far.
The salesman - so pleasant - will help you decide,
and sell you a car with a nice comfy ride.

Satisfaction

(With Keith Hollings, August 2021)

We went to the Waterside Inn today
to have a spot of lunch;
the team were very sociable,
a nice and friendly bunch.

We were shown to our pre-booked table
and ordered from the listed fare.
There was a slight delay in the kitchen,
but we didn't really care.

The lasagne dish was to die for
and the hunter's chicken was great;
when the waitress came to clear table,
we both had an empty plate.

The meal was good value for money
and the dishes were very well cooked.
No doubt we'll return in the future
to have another look.

You

(September 2021)

If you had wealth, would you be rich?
If you had a genie, would you get your wish?

If you were ready, willing and able,
would you invite others to sit at your table?

If time was on your side, would you have fun?
Or would you hide away, wait for God after all is said and done?

Because you have done all you can to this day;
you know without doubt what is coming your way.

Put your affairs in order, tie up the loose ends,
and enjoy the rest of your life, no matter what transcends.

Daybreak

(September 2021)

There are stirrings in the undergrowth,
an explosion of colours and smells,
and all of the woodland creatures
are making breakfast for themselves.

The squirrel is searching for his nuts
that he once hid under a tree,
and the earwigs, ants and spiders
are dashing to where their food might be.

The sun is rising on the land;
clouds breaking to let the brightness through.
There is fungi in a fairy ring,
their tops are clean and new.

It's not just the fauna starting their day,
the flora are joining in too,
for a good few hours of daylight
to enhance their incredible hues.

This is just a minute part
of living day by day;
Mother Nature's helping hand
will guide them on their way.

Your Little Ray of Sunshine

(October 2021)

Your little ray of sunshine
is here to make your day,
sitting right beside you
asking, "everything OK?"

I'll watch you eat your brekkie
and butter you a slice of toast,
then we will both go for a walk
just down the road to the coast.

The sky is looking cloudy,
but that wont get in our way,
'cause your little ray of sunshine
will blow those clouds away.

After lunch and an ice cream,
we'll then make our way back;
we'll have our dinner, watch TV,
and then we'll hit the sack.

So sweet dreams, my dearest
'til the morning dawns,
when your little ray of sunshine
will hold you in my arms.

Vodafone

(2021)

My partner and I went into town
as I wanted a new mobile phone.
We tried one shop with no success
and ended up in Vodafone.

Adam, the salesman, was courteous and polite;
he even managed a smile.
But when he asked me what I required,
his face hung down by a mile.

I said, "I want to buy a phone please,
but it has to be idiot proof
as I am a bit of a technophobe,
not as clever as today's youth."

He disappeared to a room out the back
and returned with a phone just for me.
He said, "It is simple to use for the everyday"
I said "does it cook and make tea?"

After a short demonstration was given,
and payment was made there and then,
my partner said I was "now up to date"
with "what, who and when".

One thing I can promise the reader:
it will not be stuck to my ear,
'cause it's too flipping heavy to handle!
Maybe one lighter next year...

Crosswords

(January 2022)

One across: a conundrum;
I get plenty of those.
A word that means *to rot or die,*
that could be decompose.

Does this word now fit the squares?
I'll have to count and see.
It doesn't work with seventeen down,
perhaps it will with three.

Acronyms and synonyms,
initials used as well...
but solve the clues to finish the grid
and everything should gel.

I've finished the crossword;
it's the best I could manage—
and I've learned a bit more
about the English language.

Aisle, Altar, Hymn

(2022)

I'll bet you're glad I sprung you
from the nursing home down the road;
you looked at me with torrid admiration
for getting you a new abode.

We'll keep each other company
and no more cooking for one—
and we'll help each other with the chores;
won't that be lots of fun?

And when it's time to go to bed,
there are no stairs to climb—
just a few steps up the passageway
to a dreamland so divine.

I'll be with you twenty four seven
as we settle down to a different life,
and every day hearing your dulcet tones:
"I can't find my grundies, where's the wife?"

Elixir of My Life

(2022)

The elixir of my life is your love for me from you;
whatever my troubles, you always get me through.
Mood swings, ailments, a bruised ego now and then;
all add up to the remedy from the heart of a gentle man.

The elixir of my life is seeing your happy face each day,
not a worry in this world, not a scowl along the way.
Take everything with a pinch of salt, like you always do;
there's no fool like an old fool... which could be said of you.

The elixir of my life is being with you forever,
spending the autumn of our years loving one another.
As time goes by we'll cuddle and hold hands,
and take each other on a journey to the promised land.

(Set to music by Bob Curd)

The Prostate Man

(With Keith Hollings, March 2023)

As I sit here looking at the grey cloudy skies above,
I'm thinking - very deeply - of my husband who I love,
'cause today he's having his bits fried with beams from all around.
That should tickle his fancy... and anything else, I'll be bound!

I know this is serious stuff and we shouldn't really laugh,
but if comedy was a medicine it could cut treatment down by half.
Cancer affects all sorts of people, irrespective of colour, sex or creed;
let's fight this disease together and stop this dastardly deed.

So gentlemen, be watchful; the signs are there to see:
getting up in the middle of the night to go and have a pee.
Go and see your doctor, it will not cost you owt;
a test will set your mind at rest and then there'll be no doubt.

If you have the illness, it's not all doom and dread;
the medics are there to help you for many years ahead.
A few weeks of radiation (which doesn't make you numb)
and a three-monthly injection with a needle in your bum.

Here comes my husband, the session quickly done;
his bits are nice and tidy and ready for some fun.
The treatment doesn't go on forever, it's over in a flash;
It's free to get on the NHS and doesn't cost you cash.

Motors

(With Keith Hollings, May 2023)

We had a little adventure
back in twenty twenty one:
my husband and I bought matching cars
from Vospers - they're the one.

And now we've gone and done it again...
but this time bought only one,
as we have pooled our resources
to save money and have some fun.

We've purchased another Ecosport,
in a beautiful shade of blue,
with all the lovely comforts inside
to make an enjoyable ride for two.

It was Matt who pointed it out to us;
said it would suit us down to the ground.
We think he was on a mission
to make himself a pound!

Sam the salesman worked on his sums,
he counted on fingers and also his thumbs.
He finally sorted a fantastic deal;
you don't know how happy this made us feel.

So much so we paid on the spot;
we've bought a car that we both love a lot.
This should last us to the end of our days;
thank you Vospers, we fill you with praise.

Still Dead, Just Checking

(June 2023)

I'm still dead; just checking!
The ground is soft and warm,
you keep bringing the flowers
and I'll ride out the storm.

I don't know how I got here,
I can't remember the occasion.
But I sure remember one positive thing:
It didn't take much persuasion.

Bits fell off and bits broke down,
well past their sell-by date;
other bits gave up the ghost
and partied to celebrate.

I'm lying here, just a bag of bones;
It's not a pretty perception.
What bits are left, the insects have had...
I hope they get indigestion!

I'm still dead; just checking the view,
making sure all is in order:
a cosy blanket of mulch and earth
and stones around the border.

A Life Well-Lived

(2023)

A life well-lived is a precious gift
of hope and strength and grace,
for someone who has made our world
a brighter, better place.

It's filled with moments sweet and sad,
with smiles and sometimes tears,
with friendships formed and good times shared,
and laughter through the years

A life well-lived is a legacy
of joy, of pride and pleasure;
a living, lasting memory
our grateful hearts will treasure.

If

(Origin unknown)

If you think you are beaten, you are.
If you think you dare not, you don't.
If you like to win but think you can't,
   it's almost a cinch that you won't.

If you think you will lose, you've lost,
   for out in the world we find
success begins with a fellow's will;
   it's all in the state of the mind.

If you think you're outclassed, you are;
   you've got to think high to rise.
You've got to be sure of yourself
   before you can win a prize.

Life's battles don't always go
   to the stronger or faster man,
but sooner or later the man who wins
   is the man who thinks he can.

About the Author

Sue Hollings

Sue was born and lived in North London until 2013 when she moved to Devon. Sue met and married her husband in 2022

Sue is a big fan of animals, art, reading and crosswords. She has even written published poetry prior to this debut collection.

www.ingramcontent.com/pod-product-compliance
Lightning Source LLC
Chambersburg PA
CBHW031531040426
42445CB00009B/479